RESCUE
A POLICE STORY

BY ALISON HART
with the assistance of
the Staunton, Virginia, Police Department

photographs by Dennis Sutton

RANDOM HOUSE 🏠 NEW YORK

The author and editors would like to thank
the police and civilian personnel
of the Staunton, Virginia, Police Department
for their assistance
in the preparation of this book.
Special thanks to Officer Kevin Pultz,
forensic photographer.

Text copyright © 2002 by Alice Leonhardt.
Photographs copyright © 2002 by Dennis Sutton.

Library of Congress Cataloging-in-Publication Data
Hart, Alison.   Rescue : a police story / by Alison Hart ; with the assistance of
the Staunton, Virginia, Police Department ; photographs by Dennis Sutton.
p.   cm.   SUMMARY: When armed robbers take hostages at a bank in
downtown Staunton, Virginia, specialized units within the Police Department
coordinate their efforts to defuse the situation.
ISBN 0-679-89366-0 (trade) — ISBN 0-679-99366-5 (lib. bdg.)
[1. Hostages—Fiction.   2. Robbers and outlaws—Fiction.
3. Staunton (Va.) Police Dept.—Fiction.]
I. Sutton, Dennis, ill.   II. Staunton (Va.) Police Dept.   III. Title.
PZ7.H256272 Hos   2002   [Fic]—dc21   99-053506
Printed in the United States of America   First Edition   May 2002
10 9 8 7 6 5 4 3 2

This book is a work of fiction, and the incidents described, though partly inspired by real events, are products of my imagination. However, the Staunton Police Department in Staunton, Virginia, and its officers and personnel are real. With their kind permission, I have used the actual names of officers and personnel. All other names and characters are my own creation, and any resemblance to persons living or dead is entirely coincidental and unintentional. Though the situations, dialogue, and actions described in the story are fictitious, they were created according to the protocol and policies of the Staunton Police Department and with input and feedback from its members.

—*A.H.*

Please note: Words printed in **boldface** are defined in the glossary at the back of the book.

0900 HOURS

9:00 A.M. A shrill beep from the alarm panel alerts **dispatcher** Cyndi Deaver-Seay. Cyndi is on duty at the Staunton, Virginia, Police Department. When she reads the paper readout tape, she notes that Painters Bank has an 05 code—a hold-up.

Sipping her soda, Cyndi sits down in front of the radio console. Because the 911 Center gets almost a hundred false alarms a month, Cyndi isn't worried. Business employees often set off silent alarms by mistake. Part of her job is to remain calm. Staunton has not

PRIORITY CODES

Dispatchers decide the importance of each call as it comes into the 911 Center. They assign a priority code to the call to determine how fast a police officer should respond.

Level C call: LOW PRIORITY

An officer should attend to the call within an hour. An example is if an officer needs to give a parking ticket.

Level B call: ROUTINE/NORMAL

An officer can arrive within twenty or thirty minutes because there is no threat of danger. An example is a "fender bender," when cars run into each other and there is only minor damage.

had a bank robbery in almost five years, so Cyndi assigns the alarm a priority level B—a routine call.

Level A call: URGENT

The officer must arrive immediately—within one to two minutes if possible. Fires, shootings, major accidents, robberies, or bomb threats would all be assigned a "level A" priority code.

Cyndi selects the police frequency and radios two police vehicle units—one that is close to the bank and one for backup. "Staunton 110, 100, 10-25 Painters Bank, 123 Richmond Road, 10-90. I will make contact with the bank," she says.

COMMUNICATION CODES

"Staunton **110, 100, 10-25** Painters Bank, 123 Richmond Road, **10-90**. I will contact the bank."

Police personnel usually talk in codes to make communication faster and to thwart eavesdropping. This is what Cyndi is saying:

110, 100: badge numbers to identify the two officers she's calling

10-25: "report to"

10-90: "for an alarm"

The officers acknowledge and head over to Richmond Road. Cyndi looks up the phone number of the bank. She dials and lets it ring. It rings over and over.

There's no reply. A chill races up Cyndi's arms. It's the beginning of a workday. Someone at the bank should pick up the phone.

Quickly, she radios the two units. "110, 100, I am unable to make contact with the bank. Have you made contact?"

"This is 110," Officer James Goodwin radios back. "I am parked in front of the bank. No one is coming to the door. The bank is *not* following procedures."

"Staunton 100," radios Bill Wagner, the second officer. "I will be responding level A from Statler Boulevard and Richmond."

Cyndi's heart starts racing. *This is serious.* Quickly, she hits the red-alert button on the radio console.

ALARM RESPONSE

Alarms notify dispatchers that a robbery or burglary is in progress at a bank. All police departments have guidelines so that the police and the bank employees know what to do in case of an emergency.

In Staunton, when the police officer drives up to the bank, he or she knows *never* to go right inside. If it is a false alarm, a bank employee will walk outside, or go to the door or drive-in window, and show the officer a special card that identifies him or her. The officer then cautiously enters to make sure everything is okay.

If a bank employee does *not* appear with this special card, the officer will immediately suspect that something is wrong.

0905 HOURS

9:05 A.M. Officer Goodwin, Staunton 110, hears the loud alert tone blast from his radio. He climbs out of his patrol car parked in front of the east corner of Painters Bank, staying behind it for cover. When no bank employee appears at the front door, his palms begin to sweat. In his two years as a police officer, Goodwin has answered dozens of false alarms at banks and businesses.

But this one might be the real thing.

He calls his shift sergeant. "110 to

27, I'm at a 10-90. The bank's still not following procedures. I'm not sure what we've got."

Sergeant Leon Sheets is already on his way. "10-4. I'm en route. Arrival time one minute. Keep me updated."

Goodwin then radios the backup unit. Officer Wagner is parked at the northwest corner. He's keeping an eye on the bank's back door and drive-in window.

"110 to 100, do you see anything?" Goodwin asks.

Suddenly, the front door of the bank bursts open. Goodwin pulls out his service weapon. A woman runs toward him, screaming, "Help! We're being robbed!"

Goodwin aims his pistol at her. "Put your hands up!" he orders. "Walk over to the patrol car!"

The woman raises her arms. At the sight of the gun, she looks frightened and confused. But for everyone's safety, Officer Goodwin can take no chances. What if the woman is one of the robbers, sent out to kill him?

The woman hurries over to him. "Face the car." Goodwin turns her around, then **frisks** her for weapons. "This will only take a second. Then I can help you."

When he's sure the woman is unarmed, Goodwin begins questioning her. Always, he keeps one eye on the bank, not knowing what to expect.

"My name's Martha Hyer." The woman begins to cry as she tells Goodwin what happened. Trying to catch her breath, she continues, "Two men burst into the bank as soon as we opened our doors. When they came in, I hid behind my desk. I ran when I had a chance. The other teller and the bank manager are still in there."

She breaks into gasping sobs. Goodwin helps her into the back of the patrol car.

His pulse is racing. This is the real thing. And it's more serious than any call he's ever been on.

0915 HOURS

9:15 A.M. Sergeant Sheets radios Cyndi at the 911 Center. "Staunton, apparently we have a botched armed robbery." Sheets is in the front seat of Goodwin's patrol car at the bank. He's just finished talking to Martha Hyer, the bank employee.

"I've got a witness who states there are two white males armed with rifles and two **hostages** inside," Sheets continues. "We will be setting up a command post at the bus station. Notify Chief Wells, Captain Dickerson, and the on-call **negotiators,** and activate the Critical Incident Response Team."

COMMAND POST

The command post is very important in a critical situation. It is located in the outer perimeter, which is close by the crime scene but in a safe area. Usually, a captain, a chief, and a shift sergeant gather at the command post to make decisions and communicate by radio with everybody involved—officers, CIRT, and negotiators. The rescue squad and fire department may also be in the area.

Sheets signs off. Two more patrol cars have arrived and are stationed at the opposite corners of the bank, securing the **inner perimeter**. Now it's the sergeant's job to get Martha Hyer to a safe place. She's the key to finding out more information about the **suspects** inside the bank.

Sheets has been a police officer for twenty-six years. He's been in a hostage situation before, so he knows how explosive it can be. If the police are going to resolve this safely, they'll need all the information they can get.

0916 HOURS

9:16 A.M. Sergeant Jim Williams, the team leader of the Critical Incident Response Team (CIRT), opens the door to the 911 Center. "What have you got, Cyndi?"

Because Williams is stationed at the Staunton Police Department, he's one of the first CIRT members to find out about the armed robbery. Before Cyndi can reply, she gets the message from Sergeant Sheets to activate CIRT.

Quickly, she sends out the 911 code that signals all the team members' pagers.

Several of the team members have just gone home, having worked all night on the 7 P.M. to 7 A.M. shift. It could take them half an hour to return to the station.

After Cyndi fills him in, Williams rushes back to the locker room. Investigators Mark Diehl and Eric Salemi are already dressing out. Questions whirl in Williams's head. Where will the team **stage**? What does the area around the bank look like? Will there be cover for his men?

CIRT UNIFORMS AND EQUIPMENT

When the members of the CIRT "dress out," they put on special uniforms. They wear battle-dress utility pants and long-sleeve shirts in gray urban camouflage patterns and combat boots.

One of the most important parts of their uniform is the assault vest. The heavy black vest is made of Kevlar—a bullet-resistant material. On the front of

the vest are pockets for all
sorts of equipment, like
a mirror to look around
corners, a high-intensity
flashlight, a tear-gas
grenade, a can of pepper
spray, wound dressings,
a smoke grenade, and a
walkie-talkie.

On the back of the vest
are two pouches for hand-
cuffs. **POLICE** is written
above them in bold white
letters for identification.

(Continued on next page)

CIRT EQUIPMENT

The gun belt not only carries the officer's service weapon—a Smith & Wesson .40-caliber semi-automatic pistol—it also holds a gas mask, extra ammunition, and a pocketknife.

The rest of each team member's special equipment is carried in a handheld pack. This includes a raincoat, a Kevlar ballistic helmet, a balaclava—a black hood made from a flame-resistant material called Nomex—goggles, knee pads, and Nomex gloves.

A second later, Officers Tom Gibson, Eric Jones, and John Craft burst into the locker room.

"What have we got?" Diehl asks, putting on his uniform shirt.

"A botched armed robbery," Williams replies. As he continues to fill them in, the five listen carefully. Already their adrenaline is flowing, charging them up for the task ahead.

"Diehl, you're in charge of weapons," Williams says as he pulls his gun belt from the locker.

"Craft, you drive the van around back. Salemi, you double-check the weapons. Gibson, load up the gas and the flash-bangs. I'll tell dispatch to send the others when they arrive."

Teamwork. Sergeant Williams knows how important it is. His special-ized **tactical team** is well trained to handle high-risk situations. Still, every time they get called out, they're facing the unknown. They must be prepared for anything.

0916 HOURS

9:16 A.M. When Corporal Doug Fry's pager goes off, he's in the middle of a meeting with a Neighborhood Watch coordinator. His stomach tightens as he reads the emergency signal.

After a fast apology, he jumps in his vehicle and radios the 911 Center. "What's going on?"

"We need you for a hostage situation," Cyndi tells him. She gives Fry the address of the bank. If he doesn't hit traffic, he can be there in five minutes.

Corporal Fry is Commander of the Crime Prevention Unit. However, in a small police department like Staunton's, he wears many hats. He is also one of the department's Hostage Negotiators.

As Fry weaves in and out of traffic, his mind focuses on the task at hand. A negotiator's number one job is to save lives. Fry knows that in order to do this he has to carefully handle a possible explosive situation so that no one— hostages, officers, or suspects—gets hurt.

As he pulls into the bus station and sees the battalion of police vehicles already there, he takes a deep breath. He hopes that he can do his job right.

0945 HOURS

9:45 A.M. "Let's roll!" Sergeant Williams hollers from the police station parking lot. Ten members of the Critical Incident Response Team are suited up. The equipment is loaded in the van.

Tensions are high. As the van drives from the police department, the team members crack jokes, trying to relieve the anxiety.

"Hey, buckethead!" Salemi calls to

the driver, Craft, as the van careens wildly around a corner. "We don't want to crash before we get there!"

"Shut up, ranger boy," Craft hollers back to Salemi. "Or *you* can drive."

Ten minutes later, the van pulls into the parking lot of the bus station. Suddenly, everybody is somber. The jokes stop. The guys unload the equipment, their minds on their mission.

Immediately, Sergeant Williams sends out a **reconnaissance** team. "Larner, you take a submachine gun. Gibson, make sure you've got binoculars. Climb up on the roof of the building next door. You should be able to

CIRT WEAPONS

The team members are trained to use special tactical weapons, which are kept in a locked room at the police department. Colt 9mm submachine guns are necessary for firepower at longer distances. 12-gauge shotguns are often used when facing an armed suspect. A Federal 37mm gas gun can shoot canisters of tear gas into a building. Tear-gas grenades can be thrown into a room to force out suspects.

The team also uses special equipment for scaling walls and entering buildings. The body bunker, which weighs over twenty pounds, is held like a shield. It is made of Kevlar, so it will stop handgun rounds. A ram, weighing thirty-two pounds, may be used to batter down a door. Ladders, pry bars, and ropes are stored in the CIRT van.

(Top) Colt 9mm submachine gun; (middle) 12-gauge shotgun; (bottom) Federal 37mm gas gun and tear-gas canister.

see through the drive-in window. Start feeding me information. If possible, I want to know where the suspects and hostages are every second."

The two officers jog off. They will be in radio contact continually. Next, Williams heads to the command post in the bus station to get **briefed** by Captain Dickerson and Sergeant Sheets. Before he **deploys** the rest of the team, he needs to know as much as he can.

1000 HOURS

10:00 A.M. Using the CIRT van for his post, Corporal Doug Fry dials the bank using a cellular phone. Sergeant Leslie Miller, the second on-call negotiator, sits on the floor beside him, ready to take notes. Using the van's radio mike, she'll also relay any important information back to the command post.

Since Miller worked the night shift, she hasn't had any sleep. Still, she's wide awake and ready. Both negotiators have been briefed so they know the "who, what, where, when, and why" of the situation. Nevertheless, they have no idea what will happen when Corporal Fry calls the bank.

Ring. Ring. Fry lets it ring ten times. Finally, someone answers. "What!" a voice snaps.

"I'm Doug Fry. I work for the Staunton Police Department. Is everybody all right in there?" The phone bangs down. Fry's not surprised that the suspect has cut him off. A big part of his job is to be patient—even if negotiations take all day.

1010 HOURS

10:10 A.M.   Outside the CIRT van, Officer Scott Bird checks and rechecks his equipment. Jumping up and down, he makes sure his gear doesn't rattle. If he has to sneak into the bank, he doesn't want to make a sound.

"Is my vest okay?" Bird asks Mark Diehl. Most of the guys have rituals or good-luck charms. Diehl and Bird always check each other's bullet-resistant vests—just in case. Next, Bird checks his ear mike. Pressing the transmit button, he makes sure the sound is clear.

Ten minutes later, Sergeant Williams comes out of the bus station, where he's been discussing the situation with the others. He tells the team members that there is no new information. "The negotiators haven't made contact with anyone inside the bank. The recon team hasn't been able to get a good look inside the bank. So here's what we're going to do."

Picking up a dry-erase board, Williams draws a quick sketch of the bank and the area surrounding it.

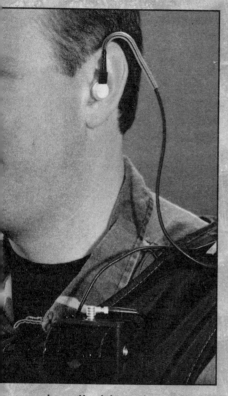

EAR MIKES

Ear mikes are an important piece of equipment because team members need to be in constant communication with each other. At the same time, they must work silently. Ear mikes have specially fitted earpieces that pick up bone vibrations when an officer talks. The vibrations travel through a wire into the officer's portable handheld radio. The vibrations are changed into words that are sent to the other team members' radios. The message travels from their radios right into their ears so no one else can hear it.

Beside it, he lists all the officers' badge numbers and assignments.

"Harris, you take Jones and Pultz and go around to the front of the bank. Find cover behind trees or signs or light poles as close to these positions as you can. Each of you needs a flash-bang and protective equipment. Relieve the patrol officers, but don't move their police cars. The suspects might view that as a threat."

As Officer Bird listens to the plan, he shifts from foot to foot with nervous energy. His equipment is hot and heavy. He's keyed up, eager for something to happen.

FLASH-BANGS

Flash-bangs are called "distraction devices." When they explode, they are so loud, bright, and smoky they confuse, frighten, and distract a person. One flash-bang gives off a brilliant light of about 2,000,000 candlepower. The light causes temporary "flash" blindness, even if your eyes are closed!

The flash-bang also makes a 200-decibel noise. That's loud enough to shatter your eardrum if you are standing within five feet of the explosion.

Flash-bangs are used in many ways to help officers arrest armed or dangerous people. They can be thrown in the air or tossed in buildings. When they explode, the suspect is usually so startled, it gives the police time to rush in and capture him or her without anyone getting hurt.

Any officer using a flash-bang must wear protective equipment. This includes goggles, a Nomex hood, and Nomex gloves. They do not wear earplugs. They might miss something crucial.

"The rest of you will be in back with me," Sergeant Williams continues. "If we have to go in, we're going to flash-bang the front of the bank to get the suspects' attention. Then we'll enter through the back door. Bird, you've got the shotgun. Diehl, a submachine gun. Salemi, the ram. Craft, you'll carry the body bunker."

The sergeant finishes outlining the plan. Questions are answered. Then Officer Harris, the assistant team leader, heads to the front of the bank with Jones and Pultz.

"Be safe," Williams calls to the three. Then he turns and faces the others. "Get ready to take up positions."

The men get in a line behind Officer Craft, who's carrying the heavy body bunker. Holding the bunker like a shield in front of him, Craft leads the train toward the back of the bank. Bird, carrying the shotgun, is the rear guard.

When Bird reaches the big tree behind the bank, he drops off. Standing behind the solid trunk, he aims the shotgun at the back door.

A hundred thoughts flash through his head. Several cars are parked behind the bank. Is one of them the suspects' getaway vehicle? You never want a suspect to "go mobile." If one of them should run for a car, Bird will have to shoot out the tires. But the shotgun has a limited range. Will the shots reach the car?

Even though the morning is cool, sweat rolls down Bird's brow. Already it's a hundred degrees under his heavy vest, hood, and helmet. Swiping at his forehead, Bird reminds himself to stay alert but calm.

His life depends on it. No matter *how* long he has to wait.

1025 HOURS

10:25 A.M. Corporal Fry has been trying to call the bank for the last twenty minutes. Finally, someone answers.

"I need to make sure everybody's all right in there," he tells the suspect. When the man doesn't hang up, Fry gives Miller the thumbs-up sign. "Is anybody hurt?" he asks.

"No, but somebody *is* going to get hurt if you don't get us out of here," says the voice on the other end.

"We can work on that," Fry says politely. "But first, I need to know who I'm talking to."

"None of your business."

"Hey, I'm Doug. I'm here to talk to you. I just need to know what to call you."

"Call me Jack. Then shut up and let *me* tell *you* what to do," the person barks. "I want all you cops away from the bank or I'm going to shoot somebody, starting with this teller on the floor."

"Jack, you know the police can't leave." Fry knows he has to stay calm, even though the man's impatient, angry tone worries him. "You've got people in there. We need to make sure everybody stays safe. What else do you want?"

"The only thing I want is to get out of here—*now!*" The phone slams down. Fry blows out a breath. He and Miller exchange glances.

At least he's made contact. Fry knows he has to keep the suspects talking. The two men in the bank need to view him as the key to getting away from the police.

Fry checks his watch, then settles back in the seat of the van and dials again. When someone picks up the phone inside the bank, he starts all over, his tone as easygoing as if he's talking to a friend. "Jack? Let's talk. What can we do to help? . . ."

1230 HOURS

12:30 P.M. Sergeant Williams kneels, trying to relieve the cramp in his leg. He's been crouched behind the retaining wall by the bank parking lot for over two hours. His knees ache, his throat's dry, his fingers on the grip of his pistol are numb. He's as hungry as a cop who's been on duty all night.

No matter how long it takes, CIRT must maintain position, securing the inner perimeter around the bank.

Williams is in constant radio communication with the command post, so he knows that negotiations are moving slowly. Corporal Fry has made contact, but the suspects aren't interested in giving up. In fact, they're demanding a car so they can make a break.

Should we get them a car?
Williams wonders. If the car only had a
quart of gas in the tank, it would stall
before it got to Interstate 81. Then the
police could move in and capture the
suspects. But the odds are they will
take a hostage with them.

And that's a dangerous situation.

On the roof of the motel, Officers

Larner and Gibson have kept Williams supplied with valuable information.

The two hostages are lying flat on the floor. One gunman keeps a rifle aimed at them. The other suspect has stayed out of sight, probably talking on the phone to Fry.

"Williams," Captain Dickerson radios from the command post, "the

INVESTIGATORS

While CIRT waits outside the bank, the department's investigative team is finding out as much information as they can about the armed men inside the bank. They check out all the vehicles in the parking lot, trying to discover which one belongs to the suspects. They can use the investigators have identified the suspects from the license plate of their car. Seems the two held up a string of gas stations and fast-food places along Interstate 81, starting in Roanoke."

Williams makes note of this new information. The guys aren't local, and this isn't their first robbery. That's not good. It makes them more dangerous.

vehicle's license plate to identify the car's owner. Since armed robbery is a federal offense, they contact the FBI. The investigators also teletype a statewide broadcast to all Virginia law enforcement agencies to see if the men are wanted for crimes in any other areas.

Williams repeats the plan in his head. Flash-bang the front of the bank, enter the back. If the team can do it swiftly and silently, they may be able to clear the bank without anyone getting hurt.

Williams contacts the other team members and reviews the plan with them. Then he checks the lucky hand-cuffs tucked in the back of his vest. They belonged to his father, a former deputy sheriff. Williams has confidence in his team. Still, it doesn't hurt to take extra precautions.

1300 HOURS

1:00 P.M. "Jack, I'm going to try and get you a car," Doug Fry says to the suspect. "But it's going to take a while."

At this point, the decision has been made *not* to get a car. But Fry doesn't have to relay that back to the robbers. He'll use any way he can to convince them that he's on their side.

"But if we get you a car, what are you going to give me?" Fry takes a sip from the soda he's holding. A bag from a fast-food restaurant is on his lap. He pulls out a cold French fry. "If I'm going to do something for you, you have to do something for me."

Fry pauses, letting the information

sink in. He can hear the guy breathing hard on the other end. The suspects have been holed up in the bank for three and a half hours. From the sound of Jack's voice, Fry knows the guy is growing increasingly anxious.

He waves the French fry as he talks. "I don't know about you, but we've been talking for over two hours and I'm getting hungry and thirsty."

"We *could* use some food in here," Jack says.

"Great. Send out one of the hostages, and we'll get whatever you—"

"You're not getting a hostage!" the

suspect says. *"But if you don't get us food, we're going to shoot one!"*

Fry frowns. Jack is on the edge of cracking up. Should he calm him down or keep pushing?

Covering the mouthpiece, Fry talks with Miller. Together, they make a decision. Fry's going to keep pushing.

Fry uncovers the mouthpiece. "You know, Jack, right now, nobody's hurt. Okay, you went in to rob a bank and things went wrong. For robbing a bank, you're not going to pull much jail time. But the minute you hurt someone, it's a whole new ball game."

"Then let us out of here, fathead."

"We're getting you a car, Jack. Or should I call you Andy? Because you're not Jack, are you? You're Andy, and you've got your friend Mike in there with you."

"How'd you know that?" the suspect demands.

"That's our job, Andy. We know you guys are young—you have no prior record. We also heard you robbed some other places. Just remember, the minute you shoot, you're going to pull ten or fifteen years in jail for sure. And if you kill someone, we're talking the electric chair. I don't think you want to die, Andy."

There's a hush on the other end, as if "Jack" is holding his breath. Fry can almost feel the tension pulsing through the telephone lines.

"So how can we resolve this without anyone getting hurt?" he continues.

"Get us a car in ten minutes!" the guy says, exhaustion making his voice shake. "Or the lady on the floor dies!"

The receiver slams in Fry's ear. Then there's silence. The phone is dead.

The suspect has yanked the phone line out. Fry knows that negotiations are over.

1315 HOURS

1:15 P.M. "The suspect has pulled the wires," Captain Dickerson radios Sergeant Williams, who's still crouched behind the retaining wall. "He says if we don't get a car here in ten minutes, he's going to kill someone. Fry thinks he's telling the truth."

Williams hears Dickerson pause; then the captain adds, "It's time to go **tactical**."

When Williams hears the command, a bolt of energy shoots through

him. Instantly, he forgets about everything but the job ahead.

"Clear the frequency," Williams
says into the radio. "We're ready to
make entry. Harris," he radios to the
officer in charge of the crew in front of
the bank, "make sure you, Jones, and
Pultz are wearing your protective
equipment. Get in position to **detonate**
the flash-bangs."

Using hand signals, Williams
directs the rest of the team to gather
behind a car parked by the back door of
the bank. When the five men are hud-
dled together, he gives everybody last-
minute instructions.

HAND SIGNALS

Often team members use hand signals to communicate silently. Keeping their gun in the ready position, they use their free hand to give the signals. If the members are in a line, a simple shoulder squeeze confirms that the signal was received.

"BAD GUY"

"HOSTAGE"

"I'm going to count backward from five. When I get to three, Harris and Pultz will flash-bang the front. On two, Salemi rams the door. On zero, we're in. If anybody doesn't understand, tell me now."

No one says anything. Salemi picks up the heavy ram. Craft lifts the body bunker. Diehl pulls his hood down.

"If we start taking on rounds, return fire," Williams adds. "But don't forget to yell **'friendly fire.'** We want to do this as safely as possible."

He glances at his men, making sure they don't have any questions. Silently, they line up behind the body bunker. An icy calm settles over the group as each member focuses his mind and energy on his responsibility.

The team's ready.

Williams nods once. "Let's do it."

1325 HOURS

1:25 P.M. In front of the bank, Officer Dale Harris presses close to the brick wall, his gaze riveted on one pane in the front window. Officer Pultz is by the window on the other side of the door, a flash-bang in his hand. Jones is behind the Painters Bank sign, his shotgun aimed at the front door.

Harris holds his breath as he hears Williams through his ear mike, starting the countdown: "Five, four . . ."

Harris pulls the safety pin on the flash-bang.

"Three . . ."

Crash! Harris throws the flash-bang at the window, breaking the glass. Immediately, he cups his hands over his ears and ducks.

Boom! The inside of the bank explodes in a burst of light, sound, and smoke.

1325 HOURS

1:25 P.M. Officer Bird grips his shotgun. The five team members are on the back steps. He's last in line, the rear guard. When they go inside the bank, his area of responsibility will be **sweeping** the back left of the building.

Boom! He hears the blasts of a flash-bang going off inside the bank and sees a blinding white light through the door's curtained window.

"Two!" Sergeant Williams continues his count.

Wham! Salemi hits the steel door with the ram. It dents, but doesn't give.

"One!" *Wham!* The second time Salemi hits it, the lock pops and the door flies open with a crash.

"Zero!" Craft surges forward, the body bunker shielding him. *"This is the Staunton Police!"* he hollers. *"Throw down your weapons!"*

Craft is inside. Diehl, Williams, and Salemi enter right behind. The air is thick with smoke. Following the others, Bird ducks to the left.

He can hear someone crying. A dark shape in the background dives behind a counter. Is it a suspect or a hostage?

"You behind the counter!" Bird shouts, aiming the shotgun at a shoulder sticking out. "Get down on the floor *now*. Throw down your weapon *now*."

For a second, nothing happens. Bird freezes. He swallows, his throat dry. *"Put down your weapon now!"* he repeats.

Out of the corner of his eye, Bird sees Salemi move to the other end of the counter, blocking the person's escape. When Salemi's in position, Bird yells, "We've got you surrounded. Give up. Slide your weapon out."

"Don't shoot," a voice croaks. "I'm sliding the gun out." Slowly, an arm appears and pushes a rifle along the floor.

"Now lie facedown. Hands behind your head." Bird moves closer so he can see around the counter. A man is lying flat on the floor. Bird covers the man with his gun while Salemi runs over and cuffs him.

Salemi pulls the man to his feet. The guy's got a medium build and has a scraggly beard. He's about twenty-seven years old, the same age as Bird.

From the description Williams radioed to them earlier, Bird knows it's one of the robbers.

Without a word, Salemi pulls the suspect out the front door. Bird lowers the shotgun. The other three people found in the bank—the second suspect, the manager, and the teller—are being handcuffed, too.

When they are taken from the bank, the building grows suddenly quiet— except for the hammering of Bird's heart.

1330 HOURS

1:30 P.M. Sergeant Williams helps a woman to her feet. Her hands are cuffed behind her back and tears run down her cheeks. Her face is streaked with dirt and she moves stiffly.

Even though Williams knows the woman is not one of the robbers, he must follow procedures to ensure the safety of his officers. That means that everybody in the bank has to be treated as a suspect.

"I'm sorry, ma'am. One of the employees of the bank will be outside," Williams says politely. "As soon as he identifies you, we'll take off the cuffs."

Williams hands the woman over to Officer Pultz, who escorts her out the front door. The other two suspects and the bank manager are already outside.

Inside the bank, Diehl and Bird are sweeping the rooms for weapons or anything else they might have missed. When they give the "all clear" signal, Sergeant Williams radios the command post.

"We have secured the building.

There are four people in custody. Get some marked units and officers over here. We want them transported separately to the police department."

When Williams finishes his call, he heaves a relieved sigh. He takes off his helmet and sticks it under his arm. Then he pulls off his hood, which is soaked with sweat. His gun belt and vest feel as if they weigh a ton.

But an even heavier weight lifts off his shoulders. CIRT's job is over, the bank is secure, and no one was hurt.

Williams checks to make sure his lucky handcuffs are still in his pouch.

Then he lets himself think about his wife and two sons and going home to them in one piece. One more time.

1400 HOURS

2:00 P.M. "Why the devil did we have to wait so long before we went in?"

"Who were those guys? I heard they robbed a gas station in Roanoke."

"How come you took so long busting down that door?"

It's half an hour later. Negotiators Fry and Miller, dispatcher Deaver-Seay, and the CIRT team are sitting around the table in the police department's conference room. It's been a long, harrowing morning. For almost five hours, the group worked the hostage situation. This is their chance to debrief—to ask questions, air grievances, talk about problems, and unwind.

When the suspects were arrested, CIRT's responsibilities ended. From now on, the police department's investigators take over. They will gather evidence from the crime scene, conduct interviews, and work with other law enforcement agencies to make sure the two suspects go to jail for a long time.

"My radio was acting up." Larner

raises his voice over the others. "Sometimes all I heard was static."

"Hey, Fry. What'd you do to make the **perp** pull out the phone line?" Diehl asks. "Hurt his feelings?"

Fry chuckles. "Nah. I told them they were responsible for cleaning up any mess they made."

Laughter fills the room. An air of satisfaction fills the room, too.

From the time the alarm panel beeped in the 911 Center to the arrest of the suspects at the bank, a critical situation was handled professionally and safely by the Staunton Police Department.

"Well, team." Sergeant Williams grins proudly at the tired crew gathered around the table. "You need to congratulate yourselves. We did it."

GLOSSARY

brief—to give out detailed information. *The shift sergeant briefs the officer about the situation.*

deploy—to place in a position of readiness. *The sergeant deploys his men around the bank.*

detonate—to explode with a loud noise. *The police will detonate the flash-bangs before going into the bank.*

dispatcher—person who works in a 911 Center. He or she takes emergency calls from the public and then dispatches, or sends out, police officers to respond to the calls and keeps in touch with the officers. *The dispatcher radioed the police officer closest to the bank.*

friendly fire—shots fired by a member of your own team, not by the enemy. *If police officers are not careful, they might be hit by friendly fire.*

frisk—to search for weapons or contraband by feeling a person's clothing.

The police officer frisks the suspect.

hostage—a person held against his or her will and used to force promises or agreements from another. *The robbers kept the bank tellers as hostages.*

inner perimeter—the immediate area around a crime scene. *The officers parked their vehicles around the bank, securing the inner perimeter.*

negotiator—a person who talks with someone to try to come to some kind of agreement. *The negotiator tried to talk the man into giving up his gun.*

perpetrator—person who commits a crime. The word "perp" is often used for short. *The police spotted the perpetrator leaving the bank.*

reconnaissance—an observation or survey, especially for military purposes. Called "recon" for short. *The reconnaissance team will check out the area around the bank.*

stage—to set up and prepare an action. *The sergeant and his team will stage in the parking lot.*

suspect—the person believed to have

committed a crime. *The police arrested the suspect.*

sweep—to carefully check an entire area. *The police had to sweep the robbers' hideout.*

tactical—used by the police and the military to express "going into action." *Sergeant Williams said to his team, "It's time to go tactical!"*

tactical team—a group trained in special weapons and procedures. *The Critical Incident Response Team is a tactical team.*

Don't miss

CHASE
A POLICE STORY

by Alison Hart
Written with the assistance of
the Staunton, Virginia,
Police Department

"Staunton, all units.
Be on the lookout for an escaped inmate.
The escapee has stolen a green Chevy,
Virginia license WEF47X."

Officer Amy Collins jots down the number.
She's writing a routine traffic ticket when a
speeding car whooshes past. Her eyes lock

on the license plate. "WEF—" Before she can read the rest, the vehicle disappears into traffic.

It's been a long, slow shift.
That's about to change. Fast.

ISBN: 0-679-89367-9

ABOUT THE AUTHOR

ALISON HART is the author of over sixty books for young people, among them the Edgar Award–nominated middle-grade mystery novel *Shadow Horse*. Because she loves mysteries and true crime, working with the Staunton Police Department was a dream come true. Ms. Hart has a master's degree in communicative disorders from Johns Hopkins University and is a graduate of the Staunton Citizens' Police Academy. She teaches creative writing and developmental English at Blue Ridge Community College. Ms. Hart lives in Mount Sidney, Virginia, with her husband, two kids, three cats, a dog, and two horses.

ABOUT THE PHOTOGRAPHER

Up until 1995, when he retired after a thirty-six-year career, **DENNIS SUTTON** was the chief photographer for the Staunton *Daily News Leader.* In the years before photography became a function of police officers, Mr. Sutton did most of the crime photography for the Staunton Police Department, the Augusta County Sheriff's Department, and the Staunton area office of the Virginia state police. For many years, he was also an active member of the Staunton reserve police. Mr. Sutton has received numerous awards from the Virginia Press Association, and his photos have appeared in *Newsweek, People,* and the *Washington Post.* He lives in Vesuvius, Virginia.